LIFE

I0157212

HAPPENS

To the Best of Us

By: Author Dorian Baham

LIFE HAPPENS

LIFE HAPPENS: TO THE BEST OF US

Copyright © 2015 Dorian Baham

ISBN-13:978-0692414576

ISBN-10:0692414576

Printed in the United States of America

Printed by Createspace 2015

Published by BlaqRayn Publishing Plus 2015

LIFE HAPPENS

...To the Best of Us

I dedicate this book to everyone who has supported my vision, and trusted me with their deepest darkest secrets. As a good friend of mine would say, "YOU ARE GOLDEN." Thank you all for believing me and #SEEYOUATTHETOP!

Sincerely Yours,

Author Dorian Baham

LIFE HAPPENS

TABLE OF CONTENTS

Believing that Life Happens...To the Best of Us

CHAPTER 1
BROKEN-TRUST

LIFE HAPPENS...To the Best of Us

BROKEN TRUST

CHAPTER 1

Who would have thought this would be happening to me? Here I am all alone and afraid of what the outcome would be. I'm terrified, I'm hurt, and I'm in disbelief. I have no one to tell this to. Who can I trust? Who will believe me? Will I only be hurt again? At this very moment all I can do is call on the Lord and ask for guidance and strength. So, on my knees I pray...

"When I am afraid, I will trust in you. In God, whose word I praise, in God I trust; I will not be afraid. What can mortal man do to me?"
Psalm 56:3-4

I'm only seventeen years old. I am a senior in high school and I'm making good grades. I have a job at a shoe store and I attend a local community college two days a week. I come from a pretty good family. Of course we've had our hardships, but,

LIFE HAPPENS

for the most part, we've always been conquerors.

I am the oldest of three younger siblings and I have a big responsibility to them. My parents work a lot, so with that being said, I care for them mostly. I had my future all planned out. Like most maturing ladies, I dreamed of all that I had already been doing plus someday being married to a fantastic guy. Yes, I was dating. I've had a "boyfriend" for two years now. He was handsome, smart, independent, but yet ruthless. We were great friends but I didn't think we wanted all the same things out of life. My parents were informed on my sixteenth birthday that I had become sexually active.

Needless to say, they weren't too happy about that. Parents aren't as naive as we would want them to be. They are very wise, due to the fact of once being us. Sex caused me to change into this woman that none of us was ready for. I went from baggy clothes and a Plain Jane persona to sexier attire. It was never over the top like these kids today because I was always my worst critic.

I was 5'3, nice sized breast, small waistline, but big legs and a huge butt. I was self-conscious of showing any skin, so I was never fond of dresses nor make-up, but I made an exception for certain occasions.

The school year passed by pretty quickly. I was blessed with all the needs of a young lady getting ready for young adulthood. Thinking about my future, I decided to make a few adjustments in my life.

Though I had become sexually active, once my parents were made aware of it, my boyfriend and I went cold turkey with our intimate activities. It wasn't much of a concern because we never really enjoyed it. We only consented to doing it because of circumstances. That caused a little conflict in our relationship. Now I had to be concerned about him dipping off with, and dating other young females.

At the beginning, he understood but as time passed and I continued to stand strong on my promise to God and myself, he then began to change on me. **–GUYS DO THAT, YOU KNOW—**

Prom was approaching! Months had gone by and I had had enough. I asked myself frequently, *why am I wasting my time on this one guy, when I have so much to offer and so much more of my life to live*? *Why, Oh why Lord*?

LIFE HAPPENS

Well, the clock was ticking and I decided on us breaking up. I followed through and it happened to be the best decision I had made thus far. I excelled in my scholastics. My job was paying off and I started making plans to move from home following my graduation. Awwwww, I had it all together. My mind was clear of foolery and it was time to start having a little fun as a young woman. I wanted to find myself, my confidence, my self-worth... And I did just that!

I made up my mind to not do Prom but my parents, friends, and siblings kept pushing the issue. UUUGGH!

LIFE HAPPENS

"Why", I asked?

They said, "Well every girl lives for that special night. If you don't you'll regret it.."

So there I was opening myself up to find a date for prom night. Though I didn't have much personal time on my hands with college, high school, and work, it wasn't too hard to meet potential prospects. I had gone on a few dates and hadn't yet felt compatible with any of them, at least not anyone I wanted to share my magical night with.

A few weeks passed...a first date, a second date and yet a third date failed, and then something

LIFE HAPPENS

unspeakable happened right before I was to give up on it completely.

_____

There I was at work one evening; my job description was a shoe saleswoman. I had just clocked in, put my purse up and was called out to the front of the store for a customer who demanded only my assistance. Well, I'd had a really long day at school with testing and I wasn't in the mood for any added frustrations. But when I walked up, I was approached by a handsome young fellow with an amazing smile. He was charming, tall, with an athletic built and much swagger. He spoke very well too, very articulate.

LIFE HAPPENS

I assisted him in a purchase of the most popular shoes in the store. That right there helped my commission to sky rocket! We then exchanged numbers and began communicating from that day on.

Two weeks later I let him come over to my house to meet my parents before a date was even an option. My parents loved him! So now I felt compelled to take him up on an offer for dinner and a movie. Two more weeks had gone by and everything seemed well. During that time span, he brought lunch to me on my job. This new hunk was doing a great job of persuading me to engage in personal time with him. I WAS SO INTRIGUED! I couldn't wait to see

LIFE HAPPENS

what a night out alone with this guy would be like. IN my mind, the date just had to go well before I popped the question. The question of what all these compromises and sacrifices were for. Which happened to be for.....? "THE PROM!" ......

Well, today's the day! And I'm getting prepared for my date. I had tried on at least four outfits, until finally settling on a knee length semi-sexy, seventeen appropriate dress. It was fitting in the waist, a little flared from the hips, and V-lined in the chest area. I was slightly skeptical of a dress on the first date, but it's what I've always seen in the movies when the girl gets the guy. Besides, if all goes well, I will be in a dress for prom, just more of a formal one of course.

Suddenly there was a knock at the door. Low and behold it was my "crush". He comes to the door as a perfect gentleman. He greets me with a rose, reassures my parents I'll be home by midnight, and opens the car door for me... off we go.

Our first stop was to go see a movie. Afterwards we went to dinner and we talked and talked and talked for a few hours having endless conversations filled with laughter. He complimented me all night long. He seemed so proud to have me on his arm.   He stood tall; he walked with his chest out, 'cause all eyes were on me everywhere we went.

Once we left the restaurant, he suggested we go meet his parents and then a friend of his and I agreed. His parents were darling, they loved me and I looked forward to meeting with them again. His friend was a little edgy unfortunately; very hospitable though. He offered us drinks and some of the weed he was smoking. To my surprise, my date joined in and started showing me a side that I didn't expect from his character. This dude got turnt up for real! He became loud, arrogant, belligerent, and then some. He started touching me disrespectfully in places I didn't approve of at all. I asked him to take me home several times. When he finally agreed, he freaked out in the car; calling me out my name, pulling me out to the car and saying,

"I knew you were too good to be true."

He ranted and raved in the car about 'Who did I think I was?', claiming I'd embarrassed him in front of his peers. In the eyes of this drug and alcohol influenced person, I now became a piece of meat dangling in the face of a carnivore. In a matter of minutes, I found myself on the side of

LIFE HAPPENS

the road fighting for my life and self-respect.   My mouth was covered, my hands were restricted, my pretty little dress was pulled up over my breasts, and my underwear were ripped and pushed to on one side while he forcibly raped me! He turned into an animal. He bit me on my stomach and chest several times. He turned me over and pinched handfuls of skin to keep me under control. I didn't know who this person was anymore. Am I getting raped by what I thought was my "Prince Charming"? I couldn't understand why this was happening to me! I cried, I screamed, but no one came to my rescue. I gave in! I just closed my eyes and prayed and prayed and prayed it would be over soon. He had committed such a violent and horrific act on me. I was weakened after it was all over. I just sat in the car and asked, "Can you take me home now?" I was in a state of total and complete shock. This punk then dropped me off a block away from my home like nothing happened and even had the audacity to tell me he'd call me later.

–WHAT THE HELL?–

What did I do to deserve this? I was dropped off in so much pain mentally, physically, emotionally. I was bleeding, crying, bruised, and I reeked of sweat and the smell of sex... I couldn't go in my home smelling like this.

As I walked up the street to my front door, all I could do at this moment was talk to God. I was clueless. I wasn't me at that moment. I was vulnerable, helpless and scared. What do I tell my parents? They trusted me! Is it because of what I wore? What do I do? Right now I just need to sneak inside, run from any questions asked about this night, take a shower and just think and pray some more for answers, for clarity...

Thank God my parents were asleep! I tiptoed into my bedroom, trying to regroup and grasp what had just happened to me. I thought I was exempt of any questioning but low and behold my little sister was awake.

My mind was telling me to keep my composure, stay calm. My sister began knocking on my door asking how the night went. Holding back tears, I responded, "Everything went well!" She wasn't age appropriate to have this type of discussion, she was only thirteen. She wouldn't go away! I never opened the door; I couldn't dare let my little sister see me this way. *I'm bruised all over, my eyes are puffy from crying, and I'm now bleeding from forcible entry down there.*

LIFE HAPPENS

As I entertained part of her conversation in hopes she'd go away, she said some things that began to bother me...

"Mom and dad thought you weren't going to make it back at the promised time. Mom said she hoped you didn't run out here like some fast tail lil girl and let that boy have his way with you...Dad said you lied to them before so you'd do it again..."

As she continued to mumble on and on through the door crack, she informed me more of what my parents secretly thought of me. In my mind, I'd thought my parents' feelings of disappointment were buried since I had made a change and a difference in my life. *I'm an honor student for*

LIFE HAPPENS

God's sake! I have a job! I'm also a college student part time! Okay, so I made poor judgment in the past with a two year relationship to take things to a more adult level, but I've tried my best to correct that! Does that give them the right to judge me off my past mistakes? Does my past dictate my future? People can change! Especially, when they let God in to help them change. I think I've done great to say I live under the influences of peer pressure daily and I still manage to have my priorities in order as a teenager.

Now I was feeling Angry! Betrayed! Un-trusted! Discouraged! *Why should I share with them what had happened to me if they have this mentality of me? I'll only be blamed, criticized, and discredited for something I nor any woman deserves, especially if it was without consent!*

All 1 was left to do was pray and put my trust in the LORD...

"FORGIVE US OUR SINS, FOR WE ALSO FORGIVE EVERYONE WHO SINS AGAINST US..."
Luke 11:4

Weeks went by and still I told no one about this horrific act. Can you believe this guy harassed me for days, not realizing or caring about what he had done to me? How can you argue with a person who wasn't in their right mind? If he did remember, he wouldn't admit to anything inappropriate happening between us. NO! It had not happened consensually. And, if my most trusted, unconditionally loving parents wouldn't believe me then there was no use in reliving that nightmare all over again.

I was worried I might be pregnant or worse; what if I had some disease. I went to a local clinic, got tested and thanked God I was left with nothing more damaging to keep that night playing in my head. I was still healthy yet very, very hurt.

That was a very trying time for me. It was very hard to overcome. In that predicament all I had was my trust and faith in the Lord. I prayed every time it crossed my mind. I prayed every night while I worked, while I bathed, etc. I was so heartbroken for sure! I couldn't understand or grasp the idea of never being believed. I didn't feel trusted. I didn't feel faith was implanted in me. However, brought me closer and closer to the Lord. I started to understand how God feels about His children when they lose faith in Him... lose belief in Him... lose trust in Him. *I am so far from God, but I too am designed in His image, and if these values and emotions don't exist for Him always, then who am I to have it?* So I thought. We are supposed to exercise these feelings. If my Father God forgives me, then my parents of physical being shall do just that. Although this is Biblical law, not everyone has self-control to self-improve. So because of the unjust, I prayed for those who needed help with self-growth; spiritual growth.

God hears all prayers and all cries of sincerity. To all of you, it may look like a bad time and bad moment for me. But I'm grateful for deliverance from EVIL. I was given a mission to take on by the Almighty. At a young age I began learning "you're not given more than you can bare..." I had things to be grateful for in that moment of despair. I harbored neither disease nor virus. I had no child as a result of it. I had no abnormality formed from it. I was blessed and highly favored!

Needless to say, I still went to the prom! And I realized I didn't need an intimate date like everyone planted in me. All I needed was someone special to share my moment with. I extended the invitation to a friend of mine and had a blast unlike any other. Times have changed and I was growing up, I had to do things for me, not to everyone else's liking

LIFE HAPPENS

The pressure my parents put on me pushed me into sacrifices, decision making, and terrifying situations that only prayer guided me through. YES LORD! I had a life to live and I couldn't let evil redirect me from a time and moment that was designed to be a memory carried with me throughout my life. I amazingly kept my faith. God gave me the strength to carry on. Though I made the mistake of never telling another human being, my God knew and that was good enough for me.

I realized I didn't have to be "GROWN" for God to come into my life and be my Savior. I just had to believe, be consistent, and sincere. Yes, I was distraught and emotionally scarred, but I WALKED AWAY WITH A FUTURE AND THIS BEAUTIFUL TESTIMONY TO SHARE.. my spiritual wisdom reassures you to "NEVER JUDGE A BOOK BY THE COVER" without knowing.

(P.S. I still never wore knee length dresses on a first date again, [laughing])

"IF YOUR RIGHT HAND CAUSES YOU TO SIN, CUT IT OFF AND THROW IT AWAY. IT IS BETTER TO LOOSE ONE PART OF YOUR BODY, THAN FOR YOUR WHOLE BODY TO GO TO HELL..."

*Matthew 5:30*LIFE

HAPPENS.........To the Best of Us

CHAPTER 2

NOBODY WINS

LIFE HAPPENS......To the Best of Us

Nobody Wins

CHAPTER 2

It's 1 o'clock A.M. and my phone is ringing off the hook! I'm skeptical of answering; I hope it's not a wrong number calling. Who wants to wake up to a false alarm? But then again, who wants to be awakened for

LIFE HAPPENS

a dreadful call? I looked over at my husband and I said to myself *it damn sure better not be any mess waking me up this time of night!*

[Ringing]

We've been married twenty-three years. I thought all BS was out the picture between us, but just as recent as six months ago I caught him messing around with another woman. We are supposed to be on a better track to a better future.

[Phone still ringing]

I'm too old for all this nonsense.

[Ringing]

LIFE HAPPENS

To give all these questions in my head some answers...

"Let me answer this damn phone!"

"Hello," I said, "Who is this ranging my phone this time of night? May I help you?" This better be good! Instead of an answer right away, I hear weeps and sobs.

[Crying]

At this point I can't even make out the gender of the person who's calling."

"Hello?"

Then I hear a voice respond...

LIFE HAPPENS

"Um hello? Is this Mrs. Davis?" I answered impatiently

"Yes sir it is..."

"Well this is Clarence Jones a friend of your son. I'm sorry to bother you but... something bad has happened... I'm calling to inform you ma'am... that your son was shot tonight and is in critical condition here at the downtown hospital's Emergency Room. The doctors need for you to come down here and please bring your husband because a blood transfusion and organ donor is needed at this present time..."

"...They'll explain it better to you once you get here. I rode in the ambulance with him because we were all hanging out tonight... Hello? Hello..."

I'd dropped the phone. I couldn't cry... I was in shock. My husband woke to the news and of course we were both distraught and terrified. We couldn't stop shaking.

Immediately we got dressed the best we could and headed out the door. I couldn't drive. I prayed the entire time going to the hospital. Along the way, I began to question God. Why has this happened to me? Why my family, why my child OH LORD? My husband didn't say a word. I definitely understood. He just kept his composure enough to get us there safely, but tears just poured down his face.

LIFE HAPPENS

Thoughts flooded my mind of my family. My son's childhood flashed right before me. I met my husband two years prior to giving birth to my son. I already had a 4 year old daughter by another man. We had a few relationship issues before he was born, but afterwards it brought our family so much closer. He popped the question soon after.

It's been a real long twenty-five years, but I wouldn't trade it in for the world. *My son is a good boy, God.* He was always an active child, yet a good one. He played football growing up and was a consistent honor roll student. He never talked back. He was always respectable, and a parents' boy. He never showed love for one over the other. He loved my husband and I equally and spent time with us both.

After high school, he went off to play college football on a scholarship. My baby got injured in his junior year and was hit with the news that he would never play again. I've always told my son to keep his head in those books because the game doesn't love anybody. No matter how hard you try, no matter the sacrifices, the bruises, the sleepless nights, once injured.. FORGET ABOUT IT! So my baby majored in Business Science. My son is very smart but his passion was football, to be in the NFL and take care of us, then finish off his life

LIFE HAPPENS

putting his bachelor's degree to use.

Unfortunately, that plan didn't work. What God had in store for him was different. He was so disappointed with the outcome of his life. He picked up bad habits such as partying, drinking, smoking, and I'd heard lately he was even popping pills here and there. My husband and I didn't know what to do. This wasn't the child we had known for twenty-one years. It was like a spiritual swap took place in our lives. I've stayed up many nights just praying for the protection of all my family. I had hoped to God he would remember how great he was, and make a change in his life. We needed him to know his worth again.

LIFE HAPPENS

In times of despair, all one is left to do is exercise their prayer rights to GOD, and remain faithful and trusting in HIM.

Well, here we are, pulling up to the hospital! I look over at my husband. My heart is racing so fast. I reach for his hand because it's not much we know to say at this time. His hands are soaking wet from sweating.

We park and began walking towards the doors. He puts his arm around me to comfort me. As the doors to the emergency room slide open, we see the waiting area was flooded with people. My daughter is here, her friends, his friends, his old team mates and coaches, my parents, my in-laws, let's just say EVERYONE is here. I don't know what I was feeling. My adrenaline rushed from excitement, fear, anger, worry, pride, disappointment, and heartbreak.

Immediately, my daughter ran up to hug me and her father. This man had taken over the role of a father in her life for so long this was all she knew. Her birth father hadn't been in her life since she was six months old and we never heard from him again. God blessed us with someone who was man enough to take on the responsibility of a ready-made family without discernment.

And here we are! Holding each other at the most difficult time we've ever had to face.

> *"TEST ME, OH LORD, AND TRY ME, EXAMINE MY HEART AND MIND; FOR YOUR LOVE IS EVER BEFORE ME, AND I WALK CONTINUALLY IN YOUR TRUTH..."*
> *PSALM 26-2:3*

The doctor enters the hall and introduces himself. He begins telling us the medical status of our child before we entered his room. He said he'd lost pints of blood. His rare type "O" was too difficult to find and my husband was needed for an emergency blood transfusion. Our son also needed a kidney and bone marrow transfusion. The tears poured from my eyes. My breaths came in short, painful gasps; I felt like I was having a heart attack. I screamed out "WHY? WHAT HAPPENED?"

As I made steps toward the room, I was approached by a police officer, a detective, and my son's friend. They wanted to inform me of the statements given to them from other witnesses.

I yelled, "Clarence please explain to me what happened to my baby!"

"Well ma'am, it all happened so fast... Jacob called and said he was depressed and wanted to hang out. He and his girlfriend had been arguing a lot lately; he'd found out she cheated on him with a football player. You know that blew him over the top, given the fact that he used to be one. So I picked him up and we went to a daiquiri shop to have some drinks and listen to some music..."

"...I didn't know he had popped some pain meds and smoked a blunt too ma'am....he...he didn't tell me the whole story. All I heard was my friend was in desperate need and I came to his rescue. I wanted my friend to not be alone because I never heard him cry out for help in this way...."

LIFE HAPPENS

Clarence stopped to clear his throat and swipe at the tears forming in his hurt filled eyes...he continued.

"...As we were standing outside just talking about the argument him and his girl had, a car pulls up and two guys jumped out. They started arguing and I heard something about him putting his hands on his girlfriend. I wasn't informed of any of this. He purposely kept that out. He knows how I feel about domestic abuse ma'am. The guys who confronted him happened to be the girl's brother and the guy she'd just started dating while with Jacob. They stated that when Jacob's girlfriend finally made the decision to leave him, he snapped! I was told he grabbed her by the throat, chocked her and smacked her a few times. His girlfriend was left with a busted lip and black eye. When she got away she ran off and called her new boyfriend who then contacted her brother..."

"...Jacob turned into someone I've never seen before ma'am. He got so angry at the guys' approach and jumped on the brother because he felt betrayed by her family. He got the best of the brother and the new boyfriend jumped in. I tried breaking up the fight but Jacob hit me too. He was whipping our ass's entirely ma'am, I'm sorry, no disrespect. But the boyfriend got away, grabbed his gun and started shooting. Jacob ran towards the guy instead of away and maybe out of fear, I guess, the guy kept shooting and that's how it all happened ma'am..." he stopped, clearly out of steam and shaken.

I couldn't believe my ears. Was this my son they were speaking of? What happened to my baby, God? He has invited the enemy into his soul and self-destructed. I got so angry hearing this I wanted to whip Jacob's ass myself. But right now wasn't the time for anger; I just wanted my son to be well. I wanted God to give me a chance to fix this. I couldn't bare losing him. He was the piece to my puzzle. I knew in my heart I could get my baby's life back on track only if I was given the chance. At this point I'd heard so much. I'd heard what the police had to say, the doctors too, but in my book, God had the final say.

The doctor approached us again and announced we were only to enter one at a time, for five minutes only for now. My husband was called off to have tests done because his blood was needed for the transfusion, so I suited up to see my boy. Paper scrubs and face mask were a must to see him. *Here I go! Lord help me, I am so weak right now, but I have to be strong for my family.*

I enter the room and my stomach does flips. There I stood at the foot of the bed looking down on my son. I couldn't stand beside him because he was flooded with tubes and machines. He was still unconscious from all the trauma. I was told a long time ago that an unresponsive person can still hear. So I immediately began praying over him, telling him I loved him. I let him know that no matter what wrong decisions brought him here, as his mother, we would get through this with God's guidance.

"MY SON, PAY ATTENTION TO WHAT I AM SAYING, INCLINE YOUR EAR TO MY WORDS. DON'T LET THE MOUTH OF YOUR SIGHT; KEEP THEM DEEP IN YOUR HEART; FOR THEY ARE LIFE TO THOSE WHO FIND

LIFE HAPPENS

THEM AND HEALTH TO THEIR WHOLE BEING..."

PROVERBS 4:20-22

I couldn't keep my eyes off him. I stood there reminiscing on words of wisdom I'd often tried to lay upon this young man. You know, we as parents can only do so much for our children. At the end of the day, free will really does exists. If a person is not ready to receive what you have to give them, it doesn't mean give up; it simply means you may have to prepare yourself for physical proof of truth to fall upon that person. And when it does, be strong enough to provide comfort to that person whom had to find out for themselves, without the "I TOLD YOU SO" speeches.

"Rest my son. Use this time to be still and listen to God's word. You are closer to him this time than any. I need you to pray in Jesus name and ask him for forgiveness, strength, healing and guidance. Mommy loves you -- and forgives you. Please don't worry about us. The focus is a better you inside and out..."

My time was up. I rubbed my son's leg and exited the room. When I walked out, I wiped away my tears and held my head high, standing in confidence that God had and would take good care of my baby. In the hallway I was greeted by my husband and the doctor. Both had a look of frustration and fear on their faces. I was confused. I asked,

"What seems to be the problem? What happened?"

Since the hall was packed with family supporters, the doctor asked if he could speak to us in private. I didn't know what more to think. I had just left my son's room and he seemed stabled and nothing had changed with his medical condition.. so I thought.

The doctor shuts the door; my husband stands beside me refusing to sit for the conversation. He looked at me angrily, all flushed in the face. I ask again..

LIFE HAPPENS

"Doc don't keep me waiting; please tell me what's wrong."

The doctor then stated..

"I'm sorry to inform you ma'am, but we took blood from your husband and ran all sorts of test to assure we weren't wrong before bringing this to your attention, but your husband's blood doesn't match your son's. Is there anything you'd like to share with the two of us so we can get your son the proper medical assistance he needs?"

I was speechless. What was I to say? My secret of twenty-two years has presented itself in the open and in the worse possible way. *Now isn't the time to lie or hold back any information, my child's life is on the line. I am so afraid right now, but I can't worry about our marriage too.. at this point, first comes first, my child.* So here goes:

"Well Doc, within the year of my son's conception, my husband and I were having some relationship issues. He was a ladies man. I couldn't get him to love me and only me for anything in this world. I was so insecure back then. I'd been in a car accident when I was young and as a result of it, 30% of my body was burned. My daughter's father left me months after I gave birth to her for another woman. I always blamed my appearance on why I kept getting mistreated by men..." I looked directly into his eyes before I said the next words..

"...My husband said he would treat me differently but he turned out to be and **do** the same as the rest. I was tired of battling my confidence. I had a coworker back then who became my best friend. We connected so well because he too had dealt with insecurities. This man was a young man with a pace maker. He understood my life and frustrations. He also understood that even though I wasn't being treated with the respect I deserved from my husband, that I was in love with him still and always..."

LIFE HAPPENS

Possibly guilt made him look away and much of the anger and tension drained from his body, causing his shoulders to slump just a bit. I continued my story..

"...One evening after an argument with my husband, my coworker and I went out and one thing lead to another; we had sex. It only happened that one time..."

There was an audible sigh from the man I'd lived with for the past 23 years and my heart felt it but the entire truth needed to be told.

"...Of course as time passed, my husband and I made amends and the coworker became part of my past. I changed jobs and we never spoke again. Later when I gave birth to my son, he contacted me. He was four months old at the time. He questioned if I thought by any chance that Jacob could be his and I denied the truth. Our marriage was so much better than before and I didn't want to lose that. My ex-coworker was heartbroken. Like I've stated, I never heard from him again..."

The strain and severity of the entire situation became too much at that very moment and I broke down...my child's one chance at life may very well be gone! It took several moments for me to compose myself and continue.

LIFE HAPPENS

"...A...a year later, I heard from a mutual friend that he...he passed away. So sir, to my dismay, there's no biological father to reach out to..he's been dead for 20 years..."

My eyes met those of my husbands and the pain, the regret I saw there was too real to ignore. I reached out to him.

"I'm so sorry honey! I never meant to hurt you. I hoped I would die with that secret. Having a child together, especially a son, was the best thing to come into our lives at that time. I didn't want to ruin that for us. Please...*please* don't push a bunch of sarcasm into my brain right now. If you only knew what I am

LIFE HAPPENS

feeling at this moment. I am blaming myself for all this. No one ever plans for their child to get this badly hurt or to pass along before them. The love you and that boy shared was indescribable. Please don't take this out on him my love... he...*we* need you! Don't let my mistake stop you from comforting *your* son. He is *your* son. You have been there his whole life. Wiped his tears, kissed his boo-boos, taught him about girls and sports, instilled the word of our Lord and Savior in his life. You can do what you want with me after this, but please hold it down for your son's sake..."

LIFE HAPPENS

My husband then squared his shoulders, gearing up to walked into the hospital room where our son laid; the door shut behind him. I could only see through the blinds what was taking place between a father and child. All I saw was my husband break down. He fell to his knees crying and begging my son to pull through. I walked away from the window to allow them some private time. Lord, I didn't know what to do, what to think, what had come over me, I was stuck, so again I prayed...

"BEAR WITH EACH OTHER AND FORGIVE WHATEVER GRIEVANCES YOU MAY HAVE AGAINST ONE ANOTHER.

LIFE HAPPENS

FORGIVE AS THE LORD FORGAVE YOU..."

COLOSSIANS 3:13

Yes I knew there were consequences behind my actions. Even though my husband had been caught a number of times over the years cheating on me, having an outside child with another man topped it all. What he had done, he didn't see as a factor; however, it was to me. His numerous affairs went out the window against my one affair that produced a child. No it wasn't fair, but life isn't fair and somehow there's always a double standard.

LIFE HAPPENS

As hard as it was, we decided to put our grievances aside to be strong for this long recovery process with our son.

&

Weeks went by with no sign of improvement. Our faith rested in the hands of the Lord. The doctors claimed they'd done all they could possibly do. Everything from this point on would have to be a waiting process. Meanwhile, we worked on us and our marriage. Even though people can make the same mistakes or one outweighs the other, the repercussion aren't really any different. It still caused mental and

LIFE HAPPENS

emotional damage regardless. The bottom line is hurt is hurt, damage done is damage done. Even though I had no reminder of his actions in the form of reproduction staring me in the face, actions that had caused me heartache, didn't mean I didn't deal with it. But I forgave him, as God forgives us all. In my case, my one time action in comparison to his numerous actions, was actually no comparison at all. My one time resulted in the conceiving and birthing of another man's baby so I guess we're even.

Though I'm hurt and embarrassed by my actions, the point is not to try to justify. I did forgive my husband and move on.

LIFE HAPPENS

Men have a tendency to not forgive as easily as women. Once again, it's an unjust double standard to life's rules.

ॐ

Two months later my son passed away. We were devastated! We gave him a proper home going and had no choice but to attempt to move on with our lives. It took us a good year to get back on track emotionally. It also took us to come together as a family, as partners, as a team to move forward. I realized living a lie had caused so much damage to the foundation we had tried to set and build upon. God gives us all time enough to come clean and confess our sins. You have to lift that weight and believe in forgiveness by confession. It may be your buried secret, but with God there are no secrets. Just like the discipline we put upon our kids, God lays upon us. Sooner or later you'll have to come face to face with your past. What can hurt little now, can be so much more painful later.

In the end, we accepted each other's imperfections and were punished for all the hurtful things we did to one another. I wouldn't say that my son died due to only my actions, but I do believe it was the actions of us both. When you don't have the will power to sit down in life because you're moving too fast, God does it for you. He'll find ways to make you focus on family, friends, and spiritual growth. These things we forget about when bills are in the way, or when jobs aren't right and cars aren't working, etc.

Each level of life has a growth period. And in between those growth periods you learn to enhance your faith, your morals, your values of life and Christ. When brought to the next level (next season) you should approach it with a bigger, better and stronger you.

"THEREFORE, WE DO NOT LOSE HEART. THOUGH OUTWARDLY WE ARE WASTING AWAY, YET INWARDLY WE ARE

LIFE HAPPENS

BEING RENEWED DAY BY DAY..."

2 CORINTHIANS 4:16

LIFE HAPPENS......To the Best of Us

CHAPTER 3

STRANGER DANGER

Life Happens.........To the Best of Us

Chapter 3

Stranger Danger

Today was awesome! I passed my CDL tests and my new job starts next week. My son had a terrific first day of fifth grade, my loan for my

LIFE HAPPENS

new car just went through, and I won my custody suit for my boy. I have had such a tough battle these last six years, but I'm finally in a better place. Lord knows I wasn't fabricating anything and God would reveal 'THE' truth, 'MY' truth sooner or later. I knew that the day would come when I could take a deep breath and appreciate the battle I've fought for so long.

My son is safe with me now and never again will I let anyone hurt him ever. I owe my victory to God, together we made a great team, and a believer out my son.

LIFE HAPPENS

"DON'T BE AFRAID, JUST BELIEVE."

MARK5:36

Twelve years ago I met a beautiful woman at a supermarket one Sunday afternoon. Sundays were the days that I went to church service, passed to check on my elderly mother, and go to the supermarket for my bi-weekly grocery purchases. On this day I was mesmerized by what I thought was the most flawless woman I'd ever seen.

LIFE HAPPENS

She had long, naturally curly hair; she was slim built with a beautiful smile. She looked familiar, but familiar in a sense of seeing her in a magazine before. I walked past her, looked up and smiled, but didn't utter a word. I procrastinated so long I finally decided to let it go. I went to the checkout line thinking *better luck next time hopefully*.

Suddenly while standing in line, I saw **her** chose the same line, coming to stand behind me. I only had about eight items and I noticed she had a basket full. I thought to myself *here's your chance..don't blow it.* So I found the courage to speak...

LIFE HAPPENS

"Uh...excuse me miss," I said.

"Would you like to go ahead of me?"

She looked at me and then down at my basket and asked,

"Why'd you ask that? I obviously have more in my basket than you do in yours..." she smiled a bit and continued...

"Usually it's the other way around," she said, giving a little chuckle.

She rightly analyzed that I was trying to be more than just a 'good' Samaritan and soon sparked up a conversation. I checked out and waited for her to do the same so I could at least help her get her groceries in her car. We exchanged names, numbers and asked the basics like "are you married or dating someone seriously". The good news was she was single and so was I.

I closed her door, we said our goodbyes, then I anxiously waited to hear from this beautiful woman. The distance to my home was about a fifteen minute drive from the supermarket and my phone had already begun ringing.

[Smiling hard]

I answered the phone so we could begin getting acquainted with one another. She seemed perfect so far. She was well educated; she was a traveling registered nurse, twenty-six years old, driving a new modeled car, no kids, engaged once before but no longer, and an only child with both parents living. In my mind I had hit the jackpot in the gamble of dating a self-sufficient woman.

❧

Seven months had now passed and my dream girl and I were still hitting if off. She stayed here in town working and would be for another year or so. Therefore, we had plenty of time to establish something greater between us.

Throughout those months, we made a lot of time for seeing one another. We committed ourselves to

LIFE HAPPENS

a Friday night of every week as our date night. We discussed the future plans we'd had before meeting each other *and* the ones we had now that we were together. On our sixth month dating mark, I asked her to go monogamous and she complied. That day I was sooooo nervous. It had been about three years prior to meeting this woman that I was living a single life. No one could have ever told me that I would be in love again. It was time though; I was twenty-nine years old and only imagined a positive love interest to enter my life to be taken seriously before I turned thirty.

I had every intention of taking things slow, but I couldn't help the feelings I was developing for this woman. The day we made our relationship official, I had asked her with a diamond watch. This watch symbolized time. Our time together thus far, the time it took to cross each other paths, how not putting a time on when, where, and how one could fall in love, and the endless amount of time I wanted us to spend together. She loved it, and I meant every word I said to her sincerely.

We had begun alternating weekends at each other's apartments which lasted until the tenth month of our relationship when we find out she was pregnant. OMG! What do we do now? We didn't plan for things to move that quickly. Of course we understood that was the chance we'd been taking in not using proper precaution during sexual intercourse.

Needless to say, at this moment, as responsible adults we had no other alternative but to fess up to the consequences of the choices we had made. I was raised to be there for the woman I admired, loved and had intentions to be with. What about our futures? What shall we do now? We asked for this but we didn't expect this so soon. We still needed time to enjoy each other and get to know each other. I did what any real man would do and I held her hand, looked in her eyes, and reassured her that we'd be just fine. I was going to be there because I was committed to her and this was possibly the WILL OF GOD.

"DO EVERYTHING IN LOVE.."

1 CORINTHIANS 16:14

As time went on, the pregnancy was coming along just fine. This was going to be a healthy baby doctors confirmed. Our relationship began having its emotional break downs, but we pulled through it. I always excused arguments or name calling during the pregnancy, since that's what the doctors told us to expect.

On a beautiful spring day, our baby was born! She delivered a healthy baby boy at 8lbs, 7oz; he

LIFE HAPPENS

was 22 inches long with a full head of hair. We were so excited, feeling so very blessed. All doubts went out our heads; all we could think of was the life we wanted to give our son.

We had a rough road in the beginning like all new parents but we were a team and we made it work. This woman turned me on by seeing how remarkable she was with this helpless little creature. Every day when I returned home from work, I would sneak in to secretly watch her with our child. I would look in on her breast feeding, singing lullabies, and changing diapers. This was a side to her I was so grateful to witness. This was everything I had dreamed of. I did my duties as the man of the household; providing, coming home to spent time with my woman alone, my son alone and them both together. It was a lot and there were times I became very overwhelmed by it all.

Two months after our son was born, my independent woman was ready to go back to work. It was a battle because she had an extreme case of postpartum depression. We found a sitter for our little bundle of joy and back to work she went.

❧

Six to eight more months into this new schedule, our lives changed completely. We began seeing less of each other and having frequent arguments. I had never witnessed nor experienced any aggression from this woman before, but now it seemed I was meeting an entirely different person.

"A HAPPY HEART MAKES THE FACE CHEERFUL, BUT HEARTACHE CRUSHES THE SPIRIT..."

PROVERBS 15:13

One day in particular was the last drop causing the pot of water over spill. Unfortunately this day was a nightmare. It had been very long and I was exhausted! I had gotten laid off without a notice. Though my significant other was back at work, it was still a bad time to tell her because of the mood she'd been in lately. She had been stationed home and not traveling with her nursing, therefore my income was much needed to balance our household. I knew when I told her the news, I wouldn't get the comforting/supportive response I felt I deserved.

As I walked in that late afternoon, I thought to myself *denial and secrets won't get me much further than what I'm assuming I'd get anyway, so I might as well quit beating around the bush and break the news...*

Here goes:

(THE MOMENT)

LIFE HAPPENS

"Hey honey, how was your day?" I asked.

"It was another day to be alive but nothing exciting, how was yours?" She stated then asked.

"Well, today wasn't what I expected either..." LIKE A MAN – "Today.. I lost my job." I said. ------ --------------------------------silently awaiting a response.

--- --------------angrily staring at me------ -------------------------

"WHAT THE HELL YOU MEAN, LOST YOUR JOB?!!!!" She yelled.

AND...The argument began!

For the life of me I couldn't get this woman to understand that I didn't expect the hand I had been dealt either. I pleaded for her to be patient with me. I suggested keeping our son home to bond more while I filled out applications online for employment. She agreed to the idea but only for the sake of saving money. My having more time to bond with my son was a situation she couldn't care less about. We were upset with one another for a few weeks before peace made its way back into our home.

Meanwhile, I was enjoying my son more and more each day. The innocent smile on his face when he looked up at me was priceless and those moments took all pain, doubt; all concerns away temporarily. I was diligently searching for jobs, still waiting for responses, but nothing yet.

LIFE HAPPENS

Two more months passed with me not being gainfully employed and the relationship with my lady was no more. I was so heartbroken, but it seemed my lack of work caused her to loose complete interest in what we had. Things weren't moving fast enough for her, so she decided to start traveling again with her job and treat me like the 'housewife' type by putting money in the account to pay the bills and take care of the baby. I had no choice but to tolerate the way things were because I was in a rough spot. I tried looking at the brighter side, like having this time apart might strengthen the relationship. Instead we grew further and further apart. I started getting the impression that maybe, just maybe, she had found another love interest while on the road. I hadn't. I wasn't about to disrespect the woman I loved and be a statistic by fathering my son then becoming an absentee parent. I loved that boy wholeheartedly and wanted to do everything right by him.

She returned home from her job about three months later with the funkiest attitude you ever wanted to witness, and a decision I had hoped not to come to past...DID! She broke up with me! She packed her things and left! *WOW!* I thought. I did see it coming, but I had hoped for a positive outcome, even more so because at this young age, my son needed the nurturing of his mother, not just me. I refused to try to talk someone out of a decision they had already acted on, so my next move was to get my mom to commit to helping me with my son while I went to school to take up a trade. I had to do something!!! Urgently!! I prayed so much. Lord did I pray.

"If two lie down together, they will keep warm. But how can one keep warm alone?.."

ECCLESIASTES 4:11

I couldn't understand what was happening in my life, but I knew there was a reason behind it; a reason that I wasn't supposed to understand just yet. All was left for me to do was keep moving forward.

అ

One day while I was out job hunting my mom called and asked me to stop at the store. I was a bit reluctant until she said it was for my boy. Needless to say, this was the same store where I'd met my his mother. UUGGGGGGHHHH! But duty called and I needed make the most convenient stop. Money was tight and I didn't need to be spending unnecessarily on gas.

As I'm going through the isles, I hear a man discussing with another guy how he was awarded grant money to start his dream business and needed good, trusting employees. I felt this was meant to be. I approached the man, introduced myself, telling him I apologized for intruding on his conversation, but was desperate, trustworthy, hungry for work, and ready to start as soon as possible. He chuckled a little because he saw the eagerness in my eyes, but the chuckle was because I interrupted. Nothing personal or discouraging, I chuckled too because I could only imagine my face when I asked. I was nervous as hell.

He then instructed me to call a number to his office and speak with his wife. His wife would give me all the info I needed. That was such a blessing! Even though I didn't have a clue yet, I was so humbled at that instant. First I didn't even want to come to this store and like always, God has used my mom to send me to his Angelic worker who was assigned to answer my prayer.

"A cheerful look brings joy to the heart, and good news gives health to the bones..."

PROVERBS 15:30

The minute I arrived to pick up my son, I rushed to share the news with my mother. Of course, my mother being a mother said..

LIFE HAPPENS

"Baby, God wants you to stay faithful and believe in Him...at your most awkward, most frustrated times in life, that is God's timing to show up and out for you!"

(Momma told you so.)

[Laughing]

Whether I wanted to hear it or not, I had to hear it and the reality was.. SHE HAD BEEN RIGHT AGAIN.

I had a new focus in life, a breath of fresh air. I spoke with the gentleman, met with his wife for all the details and the only time consuming thing was I needed a CDL. That wasn't too much to ask for

LIFE HAPPENS

I don't do drugs, I don't drink, and my mother was helping out with caring for my son. Now that I could finally see things coming together,my ex comes back in town ready to intrude and mess things all up.

[Sigh]

Believe it or not, this woman decides to take a break from traveling and stay stationary to be more involved in our son's life. I wondered with all I had, why the sudden change of heart with her. Common sense began to dawn on me because I started noticing a change in her appearance fashion wise. She now had real short hair, well groomed like a guy, stud

LIFE HAPPENS

earrings, baggy sweats and no longer beautifully manicured hands.

OMG! What had gotten into her? Didn't look like a man had. She was now *looking* like a man. I couldn't believe my eyes. This once gorgeous, out the magazine, feminine, long haired female I fell in love with was no more!

WOW! I would have never, ever imagined this. No wonder she's demanding visitation with my son; she's now in a relationship with another female who happens to want kids but can't have them.

[Shaking my head in disgust and in disappointment]

LIFE HAPPENS

I tried to be fair, though I didn't agree with this sudden change in her lifestyle and I damn sure didn't understand it. Hell, I think I loved her more than she loved me. Of course I'm not using that as a definitive reason, but for several obvious reasons, I felt I cared more in our partnership, yet that hadn't led me into a same sex relationship. I'm so confused and worried for my son. I'm the one responsible for teaching my son to be a man, NOT HIS MOTHER! *What is this*? I thought my life was headed into a happier direction.

As soon as I began believing again, this happens like life has tricked me. I don't deserve this! Or do I? I know I have to be cordial and

LIFE HAPPENS

allow my son to see his mother but I don't have to approve of her new lifestyle. At the end of the day, right is right, moral is moral, and to set an example for my son, I will agree to visitation but on my own terms.

ಎ

About five months went by and my quality time with my son was getting really weird. He was now preschool aged and could express himself very well for any reasons. I noticed when he came over the affection he once had towards me was fading. He wasn't himself anymore. He was a cheerful little boy most of his life. He didn't mind me assisting him with his baths, nor in changing his clothes but now things were different. At one point, I assumed it was because he could sense the anger and resentment between his mother and I. But as time continued, that no longer seemed a logical reason. He seemed frightened not only of me, but of my mother and most female present. It didn't sit well with me and I wasn't going to settle for his new way of being. I had had enough!

One day I decided to make a doctor's appointment to have him evaluated due to his recent behavioral changes. That day was a day to remember. I recall his mother feeling anxious about his entire visit, though she wasn't the one to take him. She seemed very agitated about me taking the initiative alone.

On the ride to the appointment, I began talking to my son, hoping to get him open up about any and everything. My son was also a quiet type. He had the typical kid personality but was very smart for his age. When I say smart, I'm not only speaking of his educational intelligence but his wise way of thinking about life and he had not yet lived much of it. Amazing kid, if I say so myself, even though his parents couldn't get it together. The way this kid thought, you could tell he was made out of true love at the time.

LIFE HAPPENS

I reassured my son nothing bad would come from this visit. Even if something brings sadness and pain to our hearts, only good could come from truth, but if kept hidden, the healing and promise of better days would only be a myth. I'm so proud of my son, he understood. But as a father and mature adult, I knew deep down inside he was afraid and didn't want to hurt either of his parents. He thought keeping secrets would keep us together because it would betray the trust of the secret giver. This was a lie!! You ought to never keep a secret that doesn't feel good and morally right to you. I then held my son's hand and prayed with him.

LIFE HAPPENS

"FATHERS DO NOT EXASPERATE YOUR CHILDREN; INSTEAD, BRING THEM UP IN THE TRAINING AND INSTRUCTION OF THE LORD..."

EPHESIANS 6:4

"Here we are son.. remember no matter what, God and I are here to protect you..." I said to my child.

We waited patiently in the reception area of the doctor's office. There were other kids there which made me feel more comfortable concerning the hands of the specialists in which I was placing my son's trust. My life flashed before my eyes. I couldn't believe the predicament I was now in.

LIFE HAPPENS

While I watched my son play along with the other kids, I questioned the reality of the life I was living. My son is here to see a psychiatrist and pediatrician to evaluate his mind and body. As his father I just know something is wrong.

OFF HE GOES…[Sighs]

ॐ

An hour passes and then, "Excuse me sir, can I see you in my office? Your son is just fine playing in one of our toy confession rooms. It's a room were we find a more comfortable way to get the kids to open up in conversation. Please follow me." The doctor said and off we went.

I sat down nervously as the doctor closed the door behind me and began listening with all ears. I couldn't fathom what I was hearing. I was informed that my son's mother's new friend (girlfriend) was sexually molesting him! OMG! This had to be a nightmare. I can't believe this! I'd known in my soul something wasn't right. I cried so hard it felt *my* heart was going to give up on me. I was so hurt, so ashamed, so disgusted, so angry, so confused, so empty; just so damned fed up! I felt I had let my son down, like I didn't protect him. I blamed myself for losing my job. I blamed myself for being so submissive, I blamed myself for his hurt so much, I didn't know what to do nor think of myself. *How could I let this happen? Why would God let this happen?* I felt like dying, but I knew more than anything my son needed me to protect him like never before.

I was somewhat upset with him too because I wondered why he hadn't trusted 'daddy' enough to tell me what was going on. I thought to myself *I could have put a stop to all of this if only he would've spoken up the very first time.* I WAS SO FRUSTRATED!

The doctor gave me a moment to myself to calm down. He wanted me in a suitable state before I saw my son again. I really didn't know what to do. *Here I was still trusting the woman who had put a dent in **my** life with **my** son's life. The very woman who didn't do right by me in my life has now brought wrong and pain into my son's life!* I felt like choking the life out of her the first time I laid eyes on her, yet in reality, I knew it wouldn't solve a thing. *It'll only gives her what she wants and that's to make a fool of my life because she made a fool of hers. She envies the fact that despite my downfall in employment, I still held my sanity and held my ground strongly as a father.* That thought right there was enough to go on in order to keep me strong for my son. I may have been angry but I was far from stupid. *My mission and goal shall remain the same; to continue my classes and past my test to finalize this job offer and take my son on to a better life. What's going on with her is none of my concern; my concern is him, and as his father I will lead him by good character and as a Christian. I will hold my child and comfort him. I will teach him to pray for his mother's misguidance. I will show him how to overcome obstacles in life and who is responsible for changing victims into victors….GOD!*

We have been blessed in the mist of the storm. My mother has

LIFE HAPPENS

been there to play a motherly role to my son until we are blessed with a positive, more level headed woman to enter our lives. Our life may not be storybook, fairy-tale perfect, but God has written a beautifully triumphant ending that was only designed for us, and for that we owe Him to live it to our best ability. God makes no mistakes and though some chapters in our lives hurt like hell, REMEMBER HE ONLY GAVE YOU THAT ROLE BECAUSE YOU WERE BEST FOR THE PART.

I open the door and there is my son with a smile of relief upon his chubby little handsome face. I stood there and literally I could see him standing taller, brighter, more confident, with a glow that only stayed long enough for me to see, then faded away. I guess that was my confirmation of an Angel protecting my son all along. The molestation wasn't as devastating as it could have been, but one inappropriate touch is all it takes to be too much. I extended my arms, my son jumped into my arms, and we hugged each other tighter than ever before. I promised him I would always protect him and he'd never be scared again. If ever he feels comfortable to tell me, I will always be here to listen.

LIFE HAPPENS

From the doctor's office the authorities were called. They had papers written up through Child Protective Services to immediately remove my boy from the presence of that woman permanently and to move forward with a full investigation and charges. Yes we knew it wouldn't be easy, but it was a fresh start towards our new life together.

"HOW GREAT IS THE LOVE THE FATHER HAS LAVISHED ON US, THAT WE SHOULD BE CALLED CHILDREN OF GOD!" 1 JOHN 3:1

LIFE HAPPENS......To the Best of Us

CHAPTER 4

Home Is Where the Heart Is

Life Happens.........To the Best of Us

Chapter 4

Home Is Where the Heart Is

...After all the sacrifices, after all the hard work I put into my career, my family, and my friends...

LIFE HAPPENS

"I WAKE UP LIKE THIS!?!"

It has been a very long two years. I went from having it all to having nothing at all. *How did I end up here?* I ask myself this question every day. Of course I am grateful for the air I breathe and the opening of my eyes every time the sun rises, but I still don't understand why I was dealt this hand when I thought I had it all figured out.

My life today consists of handouts and looking for dry spots to lay my head. I can only bathe when a chance opportunity arises.

I AM HOMELESS!

LIFE HAPPENS

There are shelters that provide room and board on a first come, first serve basis. In this city, there are more blighted houses than those in active use to accommodate those less fortune. There are places that allow showering but not frequently enough. There are facilities that provide meals for people like me, but they often run out of food. Even when there is enough food to go around, it still may not be a feeding day for us because certain food we cannot eat due to health reasons. Clothing is donated and issued out but keep in mind, we can't travel far with an abundance of belongings and, of course, there is nowhere to store it all. Most days you only take what gets you through that day. Not too often we are given options of requesting clothing and our shoe sizes because no one really cares that much about whether it fits.

The mentality of donors is that "WE", meaning people in my position, should be glad to receive ANYTHING given to us when that's not right. We are human too, just in a bad season, on a rough road, often as a result of poor decisions and keeping the wrong company.

Sometimes when you see me standing on a corner asking for change, it's because I would like to wash what I have. I have good morals, manners, and was very tidy with my belongings since a child. My mom instilled in me how to take care of my surroundings and my belongings. I brush my teeth in public restrooms as much as possible. I try sparking conversations with people, but they never really give me a chance. Instead, they pity me and that's not what I want. I'm A man! ALL I WANT IS A CHANCE TO CHANGE MY SITUATION!

❧

I have walked miles to look for jobs in size 10 shoes when I really wear a size 13. My feet are now in constant pain from arthritis, which doesn't allow me to walk very far. I have had my shoes stolen from me while using them as a pillow when I could barely keep my eyes open any longer. I DON"T DO DRUGS! But yes, there were times I wanted to give up and I entertained the thought using. I know that would only make my situation worst, so I pray every day. I also attend a 7am mass at a neighborhood church to keep my faith. If anything, I know I can always talk to my Lord and Savior. I may not understand my life right now but I am accepting of His plans for me.

Yes, I do drink every so often, reason being it gets so hard out here sometimes; I just need to numb the emotional, mental, and physical pain somehow. I've never stolen from anyone a day in my life, not even with being down on my luck. You should see my home. I'm talking about where I lay my head at night nowadays. I met a guy out here on the streets who's known for making the best shelters to protect u from bad weather. You wouldn't believe the creativity!

"WHEN YOU STRIP A MAN OF EVERYTHING, HE'S CAPABLE OF MAKING SOMETHING."

We all somehow have to make a living and are all trying to escape our situations, so of course this guy costs. But in life what doesn't? So sometimes when you see me asking for a little assistance, it's not to get over on you, it's to pay off a debt for

LIFE HAPPENS

a better way for myself and whomever else I can bless with shelter. Due to weather changes my skin suffers. It cracks in places you wouldn't imagine what with not being able to cleanse it or take proper care of wounds I've endured along the way. My heart isn't in the greatest state. I am a man with sexual desires who's afraid to fulfill them because of my uncleanliness. I am afraid of diseases, I am afraid of viruses, I am afraid of more need for well-being. So the thought of any type of physical intimacy is pushed from my mind. I have met some wonderful people with amazing stories like myself and though I have lost a family, I have gained one just as real right here on the streets.

We protect one another from danger and harm. We share the small meals we hustle throughout the day. We sleep in shifts to guard against the street demons so we can at least rest peacefully for the time we do have. I suffer from back pains due to kidney issues from not being able to get fresh drinking water daily; a lot of us do. There are no fountains around the city to get free purified drinking water. Everything Costs! Sometimes after spending the little money I am blessed with from strangers to build my fort to shelter myself and my belongings, I lose it all. I can elaborate.

LIFE HAPPENS

After searching high and low for a safe haven, the moment I spend time away from it, the city is directed the clean the streets and without warning all the things I've accumulated are removed and dumped. Now back to square one. Each day it feels I'm starting over from scratch. Could you imagine that? Every day of your life is erased, and each day you're at the bottom. That's very hard living. Sometimes I have to put on all the clothes I have just to assure I have something to wear. If it's not due to trying to keep warm, it's due to others like myself being in survival mode and wanting what you have. It's very uncomfortable. Imagine always going to bed fully dressed. Not an easy thought huh? Even though my life is this way now, it won't always be unless I give up on myself and the Lord above. But giving up is not an option. I'm no quitter! And believe it or not, though I'm helpless, I am not hopeless and for that way of thinking I AM HAPPY.

"For I know the plans I have for you, " declares the LORD, "plans to prosper you and not to harm you, plans to give you hope and future."

Jeremiah 29:11

Let me explain to you how this all happened…

LIFE HAPPENS

Three years ago I was in the prime of life. I had the storybook lifestyle, but I didn't appreciate it like I should've. I had an awesome career; I owned my own contractor's company. I did everything from restoring old buildings, painting, flooring, lighting, the whole nine yards. I had a beautiful wife of 11 years with three beautiful kids. I got so caught up in working and the money that I was bringing in, I forgot about the things that were most important. I was so exhausted that I began losing interest in all that really mattered and the reasons why I strived so hard. I stopped going to church with my family.

LIFE HAPPENS

As a result, I didn't realize that they were building a foundation with God that didn't include me. Sure they were praying for me, but with free will being a given, I couldn't receive the blessings without being on the same receiving page as my love ones. Everything started falling apart and I was too selfish and stubborn to stop and deal.

My parents were elders and had been married for 46 years. For several years they had been dealing with illnesses and I was the only child to care for them. My wife and kids took on the responsibility of nursing and nurturing my sickly parents. I would occasionally step in to help out, but I did it with attitude. It disturbed me whenever I was stopped from working, because I loved what I did and I loved whom I did it for. However, it never dawned on me to think that my priority to provide financially for my family was a hindrance to our love and devotion to one another. I take full responsibility for my actions. My wife tried, my children tried, my parents tried, even my employees and close friends tried talking some sense into me, but nothing worked. When your mind is made up and you feel you're the only outlet of financial relief to those you love, you tend to unknowingly grow more love for the act of providing than for those you're providing for. When the ones you love ask you to slow down, they definitely have their reasons.

"If two lie down together, they will keep warm..But how can one keep warm alone?"

Ecclesiastes 4:11

Months went by as things continued to worsened. My wife became more frustrated than ever with my actions and all that was happening around me. She decided to take the kids and go visit her own parents for a undetermined length of time. I was heartbroken. The reality check brought on by her actions only made me angrier, yet I started realizing my loss. I'm not bitter

LIFE HAPPENS

towards her because I was warned several times and did nothing to correct my behavior. I know she loved my parents dearly, but in all fairness THESE WERE MY PARENTS, SO THEY WERE MY RESPONSIBILITY. I took advantage of a good, supportive wife. I depended entirely too much on her to take on everything and as a result, I think I lost her.

Once I took a deep breath to see all that was going on, I put my emotions aside to tend to what was being neglected...MY PARENTS. I decided to take some time off to go spend with them. At this time, I felt like a kid again. It was selfish of me, but I needed my parents to give me advice on what had gone wrong in my marriage and how to hopefully gain it back.

When I arrived at my parent's home, I began to cry. The house was a wreck! The yard was unkempt. The siding was falling, the foundation was uprooting and garbage was thrown along the alley ways of the house like rodents had gone thru it. I was appalled, but I also got angry with myself immediately. Seeing this, I now understood with no doubt my wife's actions and frustrations towards me.

As I walked towards the entrance of the home, I began picking up trash along the way. I

LIFE HAPPENS

knocked a couple times, rang the doorbell, then used my key to enter. I called out for my parents and there was no answer. As I proceeded towards their bedroom I heard weeping and sobbing. My mother was worn from crying while lying next to my father who seemed to be unresponsive. I stood in total shock, embarrassment, hurt, anger, and disbelief. I cried hysterically to my mother asking her what happened. She could barely grasp her breath to tell me. There was no phone near them, the cordless phone was dead, and no one had checked on them in 3 days. I immediately took out my cell phone to call for help, while holding my mother's hand and kissing my father's forehead. My mother than wept a few words and informed me that their electric had gone out for a couple days and dad lost his oxygen from his tank. He was too weak to walk far and my mother is disabled and unable. She horrifically watched the man she had loved for nearly 50 years die before her eyes, unable to help him. She was distraught!

The LORD GOD said, "It is not good for the man to be alone, I will make a helper suitable for him."

GENESIS 2:18

LIFE HAPPENS

When the ambulance arrived, both my mother and father were removed from the home. Sadly my father was pronounced dead while sent my mother into a state of shock and total depression. She was admitted to the hospital and it was then that I learned at the time of my father's death, my mother had suffered a mini stroke. I was so lost. *I am the only child and my wife was my back bone. It's time to give her a call and inform her of this sadness.*

"For this reason a man will leave his father and mother and be united to his wife, and the two will become one flesh..."

Genesis 2:24

LIFE HAPPENS

Calling my wife only made me feel worse. It wasn't the time for the blame game but I deserved it. She cried and cried and hung up on me after telling me she never wanted to see me again. She called me selfish, self-centered, and so many other names that I refuse to own up to. *Okay, okay, I'm a man so I'll except the backlash but now isn't the time. I just lost my father whom I missed saying goodbye to and now my mother isn't doing too well. What is one to do besides pray for strength, wisdom, courage...* so I did.

Dear God,

I know I've been more than a fool lately and I have come to pay a very costly price. I am so sorry God and I

LIFE HAPPENS

humbly and desperately ask for your forgiveness. I need you God. I come before you to take full responsibility of my actions so you can guide me on a righteous path and correct my human nature. I receive your punishments God, just please no more, I can't bare no more.

Moments later, I entered my mother's room just in time to witness her last breath. I fell to my knees! God had given me the pain my mother witnessed with my father. I had to watch her take her last gasp of air helplessly just like she had gone through with my father. I felt like I was 2000lbs. My body was so heavy with burdens.

LIFE HAPPENS

I went back to my parent's house and did what I had strength to do. I cleaned what I could as I cried over memories and memorabilia. I knew they wouldn't live forever but I pictured things being so different. I wanted what they had. I wanted the longtime friendship, family, trust, respect, and communication with one another. It was admirable and old fashioned. I had found those qualities in my wife, but I messed it up. My father always said, "MAKE TIME FOR YOUR FAMILY, SON." But with 3 kids in comparison to their only having one, I didn't think he understood why I worked so much, and I didn't understand why he didn't. I thought I was giving my family the world, but their world was nothing without me in it. Now I get it. Now it's too late.

> *"It is God who works in you to will and to act according to his good purpose..."*
>
> *Philippians 2:13*

A week passed and I was able to see my wife and kids at the funeral. She consoled me and assisted in taking care of things for my parent's home going, but what we had just wasn't there anymore. I could only respect her decision about what was best for her and the kids. We then found time to have a sit down discussion about our future together. There was none. Just because I felt alone and hurt at that very moment didn't mean that I was guaranteed to change who I had been for so long overnight. Her thoughts of me were wise. There was no way it was fair to make promises under this kind of stress. The reaction of my kids was also heartbreaking. I then realized I had been such a disappointment to them so long that my absence in their lives was already an established fact. It hurt, it hurt like hell, but I AM A MAN and I brought this on myself. Though I didn't like it, I stood tall and received all consequences that came along with my actions.

I had lost everything I'd known all my life, most my life, and what I desired in life. Now my plans had changed. God's plan began to takeover. I could have had a beautiful ending if only I would have listened to the signs. If only I wouldn't have taken those I love for granted. I wanted so much control over my life, that I had overlooked the lessons along the way. Now where does that lead me? Where do I go from here?

My answer comes a few months later when I wake up in a hospital from a stroke. Now I have nowhere to turn, no one to talk to, and nowhere to go. My home is packed away with my wife and kids. She won ownership of my business and due to my hospitalization; someone else has been assigned to take over. I have been noted as incompetent to carry on in my line of work. At that very moment I chose to give in to the 'MASTER'S ORDERS'.

On the day of my release, I had no more fight in me. I was shown the power of prayers in me and against me. Though I had no direction, I gathered up my belongings and walked out the door into a new path directed for my life. I made the decision to walk in faith and let Him lead me to what's now destined for my future. That choice brought me to where I am now. And where I am now is without a permanent roof over my head, all alone with myself, my thoughts, and my God. Believe it or not, I'm ok with that. I may not deserve every

LIFE HAPPENS

hardship I'm experiencing but I do take responsibility for most. The family I have lost and left behind can never be replaced. I keep a photo in my wallet of our happiest time together and that right there keeps me strong and determined. I know this isn't the end. But I do know I have to walk this walk to learn and appreciate when I'm blessed with love again. I have made peace with myself; I can also love myself through this test. Today I carry no weight of feeling sorry for myself. I'm actually a better person now that I know and understand what I have lost. I also realize that even though I may feel ready for deliverance, or that I am tired of this way of living doesn't mean that God is ready to relieve me of it. The reality check that was given to me so harshly was that, His timing can't be timed! So meanwhile, I await my turn. Home lies within my heart while I take in daily lessons to be an inspiration to those headed in my direction.

"PRAY CONTINUALLY..."

1 THESSALONIANS 5:17

Life Happens..........To the Best of Us

Chapter 5
Lost ID

Life Happens.....To the Best of Us

Chapter 5

Lost ID

"Um excuse me ma'am, do you have these in a size '34 '32? I'm usually a size '32, but I like to have a little sag in my swag. (Laughing out loud)

I like the way these fit. They are giving me life, baaaby!

Ok, Ok I'll take this pair of jeans with that banging ass chain that reads "DOPE BOY!"

Run that by me again baaaaaby.

You said, "$376.14?" No problem, money ain't a thang ma. I got that.

Before you give me that receipt, you make sure to write your name and number on the back of it.

LIFE HAPPENS

Let me take you out sometime and show you how a woman should really be treated.

It was nice meeting someone as beautiful as you, thank you sweetheart, hope to hear from you soon.

You've made my day..." (wink,wink)

That day changed my life forever. That was a day I was feeling myself and foolishly extended an invitation to the wrong situation that ruined my family.

LIFE HAPPENS

I had a normal childhood. I grew up in middle class living with my biological parents. I played sports most of my life and I am musically inclined. My mother was a sports commentator and my father played music. He was a drummer to be exact. Sounds like two totally different people who had nothing in common, but in all actuality they were inseparable. Even though they always seemed happy because of their career choices, they were both constantly around the opposite sex, and at times, it became very challenging to stay faithful and committed to one another.

My dad traveled the world. He played for a band that was very popular and successful. My mom, on the other hand, always had these fly ball players around her. These guys were paid and full and well rounded. They both created great relationships with their colleagues and our house always stayed full with invited and uninvited guest. The upside to that for me was being considered a fortunate kid to always be in the presence of celebrities. I was brought up to treat them (celebrities) like you and I; as normal folk.

My friends admired my lifestyle and upbringing, but little did they know I had sometimes wished for a more normal life. I mean it was cool and all, but we never stayed in one community for long too long, therefore, I never knew what it was like to have long-time, long-term friendship. I was programmed to love and let go. There were so many unresolved relationships I had left behind.

There weren't many women who could relate to my mother's lifestyle. She lived her life almost like a man. She had mostly male friends and so did my dad. I grew up admiring and only watching the accomplishments of men mostly. I had witnessed, even in my dad's career, a woman's hurt and their naive state of mind when it came to the love music. Most of what I had grown up seeing was the heartache and pain ball players and musicians caused to these women and families they loved. They would only lavish these women and children with trips, big houses, fancy cars, and shopping sprees, to leave them behind lonely and miserable.

My mom on the other hand, couldn't relate to those lost ladies in love because she lived in the fast lane herself. Therefore, there were women who were inspired by her and very envious of her as well.

With no one to ever give me clarity on the life choices I'd witnessed, I became very confused. I didn't know who to love, how to love; I didn't know what love truly was, nor did I ever think I could have it for any worthwhile period of time.

ॐ

    I am off to my first year of college and I'm feeling some type of way. I'm studying Communications. I chose that major because I felt my family lacked it and maybe in order to mature, I needed to get a grip on verbal expression.

    Upon settling in my dorm, I met up with some friends from high school, heading for a party we'd been invited to attend. It was the first party of the year to welcome all the freshmen. Of course I had to be the freshest thing at the party. So off to the mall we went! You already know how I get down. Money ain't a thang is how I was brought up.

While shopping I met the prettiest young lady I've ever seen throughout all my worldwide traveling . I couldn't help but ask her out. She complied. Now there's only one problem. I have to decide on which life I want to live being away from home. I say that to say this, although I live my life by what you see before your eyes, I'M REALLY A WOMAN!

Portraying a man has protected me from hurt and given me strength in my heart I figured no normal woman could handle.

LIFE HAPPENS

It all started when I was about fifteen years old. Back then I had my first heartbreak by my first boyfriend. That was a pain I never wanted again.

When my boyfriend cheated on me with another girl who was then sexual active and I wasn't, it just destroyed my mindset. I had a flashback of all the women I witnessed hurt by men and their greedy need to have their obsessions fulfilled at any price. Not understanding much, only going by what I had seen, I concluded that all men did was confuse the hurt with hurt. (Except for my daddy.)

LIFE HAPPENS

It was then that I realized everything I went through, my best friend was always by my side. A best friend was what I wanted in a relationship because I saw that in my parents relationship.

Needless to say, I always heard mom and her friends express that God doesn't make loyal, trusting, well respecting mates any more. So I took thoughts and teachings into my own hands. Therefore, I became curious about taking my love for my best friend to a companionship level; a romantic emotion began to emerge for her. With her not wanting to lose our friendship, she agreed. We dated until the summer before our senior year in high school. I began changing my appearance took on more of a masculine look and the more comfortable I got in my transition of living as a man, the more my relationship with my bestie faded. She loved me for me, she sacrificed for me, she was seduced by the female me, not the male me.

After growing up a little and understanding that the choice we'd made came with a lot of misguided confusion, we decided to only remain friends but explore in different places with different people. She assured me that there will come a day that I would be sorry for not being me. She tried to get me to realize that I could be loved just being me, without a misleading cover. My personality and character make-up was and still is phenomenal. I respected her opinion, but for me it was more comfortable if I portrayed masculinity and dated women, then being myself.

I had insecurities that no one could help with BUT ME... when I was ready to confront them. My life was a result of having parents that were too consumed with success to really pay adequate attention to me; especially during those formative years. They were good parents but they weren't always around to guide, raise, assist, and explain growing up to me; I learned a lot from trial and error.

LIFE HAPPENS

"Lord Jesus, I'm really confused. I really don't know why and I don't know what to do and I can't help the way I feel. So I'm coming to You...

Lord Jesus, speak a Word to scatter the darkness in my mind and heart. Burn away the clouds of uncertainty. Shed a ray of Your Divine Light With its healing rays to set me straight. My mind, my heart, my body, my soul,

I give to You...take control.

Jesus, in trust in You.

Amen,

Anonymous

❧

Now that I'm in college things are so different. I now see a world in which my best friend was trying to prepare me for. Here feminine girls are accepted as being lovers openly. IT'S COLLEGE!!! It seems everything goes. No one passes judgment about chosen lifestyles here. I assume this is the transitional breakthrough in your life where you give it all the good and bad you got in order to know where you're headed. Experience is the only way to learn confirmed decision making for future goals and planning of what to become and what to not become. The only downside to that type of trial and error is hoping and praying that the mistakes you make trying to find yourself don't cause you your freedom or your life.

What I wasn't wise enough to put together was that I could get hurt in more ways than just the heartbreak I was avoiding from men. I was taking chances of sexual transmitted diseases, getting caught up in lies and deception, etc. I never thought of ALL the consequences, I only thought selfishly about my own taught behavior and desperately trying to avoid heterosexual love.

On the night of the party at one of the frat houses, I entertained the young lady I had met earlier that day from the mall. Keep in mind she was under the impression that she had met a handsome young fella. I usually don't disclose to people when we first meet that I am actually a female because I was confused of what I'd become. I was confused of whom I'd choose to live my life as for the rest of my life. If only I had made a magical connection with a woman that gave me the assurance that this way of living is what I'm happiest with, then I'd open up in sharing my story of why and how I had gotten to this point.

This young lady was remarkable. She was funny, beautiful; both book smart and common sense smart. We talked all night about our families, our college majors, where we would like to see ourselves in the future, and then the talk of kids came into question. That was a question I never really asked myself. Good question though. I had to wonder and ponder the idea of being a parent someday. Of course, this little lady wanted it all. But there was no need to get out of tune now because she and I had just met. No telling if tonight will be the last night knowing each other, but, on the flip side, I kind of liked this girl.

She had an inviting spirit and she was very easy to talk to unless I was just getting better at my communications major. We had nothing in common but I liked that even more. I thought being so different like my parents were would always give us something great to talk about. My folks always had stories about their days that actually interested one another. That was the key to great friendship within their relationship. It's one thing to have different lifestyles and careers, but to honestly be interested or intrigued by it is another. No one wants to come home and talk to the wall. Everyone wants to be heard; especially by their loved ones. It gives off a sign of genuine care and concern. That attention leaves no room for infidelity. And that was something that I admired.

Most people would say that I was too young to be thinking seriously about a relationship, but in reality I was just ready to learn. I was ready to know what life I wanted to live and who I wanted to be. I didn't feel great about using people to test my sexuality but I just had to know who I was.

At the party we jammed! The party was hot! It was one to remember. This was the first welcoming party into the first semester at our first year in college. Though I was nervous, I played a role of confidence in my masculine appearance. I don't think anyone actually knew my real identity. But of course I share a dorm room with someone who will.

For now, I introduce myself as a male with a feminine name that has been common for children over the past 20 years. Who would've thought some kids would actually grow into their names? Choosing to live their lives as the opposite sex.

I got away with it until sophomore year in college. Me and the beauty at the party hit it off. We'd been having an monogamous relationship consisting of friendship, dating, kissing, hand holding; absolutely no sex has happened. I am now at a point where I trust this girl extremely. I respect her so much. She has been nothing but loyal to me, and now I'm beginning to feel awful about deceiving her into thinking she's being protected and loved by a male. I want to tell her the truth but I don't know how.

LIFE HAPPENS

She has given me an ultimatum. My parents are having a big anniversary party and they want me home for it. I don't want to leave my girl and she doesn't want me to go without her. Thinking like a female, she's ready to meet the family. It's been two years now. *So what do I do? Do I ask my parents to play along? Do I tell her before we leave or when we get out there?* If I tell her now, she won't come. I don't know what to do. I don't know how I let this secret lie for so long. My parents won't pretend I'm someone I'm not. They didn't agree with my lifestyle choices before I left for school. They both thought that this would be a phase I would out grow.

LIFE HAPPENS

In my parents' minds, bisexual, bi-curious, or even homosexual relations in college was a fad for late teens-early adulthood. But there was no way they'd accept me showing up as a guy. In my mind, all I wanted was for this to go smoothly and normally with no mistakes. I would love to just go visit home with my girlfriend and come back an even happier camper to a normal life.

In real life though, I'm not sure that will happen. So we pack our bags anyway and head out, without me telling her anything.

જ

LIFE HAPPENS

After a four hour drive, we arrive at my parent's house. I hadn't seen my parents in what seemed like forever. When we pull up, she is so in awe about where I lived, where I came from. Meanwhile, I'm thinking and wondering *what the hell do I do next!* I'm nervous! We walk up to the door and I yell out to my parents; they are in the yard getting things together.

When they see me, they give me a look only a child would understand from their parents. I gave them a look back and unspokenly they had an idea of where not to go with this. After all it was a day of celebration, the judge and jury was out on bringing up anything that would sabotage the day's event. I introduced everyone and all was going well.

More people started arriving, yet no one seemed to pay me much attention what with today's trend for young people. She and I didn't display any physical emotion towards each other, she was a little nervous, so we didn't raise any eyebrows at that point. I thought I had gotten away with having to confront the truth of the situation. It wasn't the time or the place. I felt relieved and it was just a matter of time before we were headed back out on the road.

Until…

LIFE HAPPENS

Until my bestie showed up. My first homosexual relationship, my high school sweetheart and best friend walked through the door. Right then and there my mouth felt as if it disconnected from my face. Of course we were still friends, but I never let her know about my new girlfriend. When we would talk on the phone or write letters, I would downplay my lifestyle and deceive her by having her think I was coming up out that confusion. She would see pictures of me but I would never be fully dressed in my everyday clothing choices. My social media sites are under alias names and we weren't friends on any of them. Therefore, there was no real connection besides talking. I felt by making frequent calls, she wouldn't dare have a reason to second guess what I had been feeding her. Being a communications major, speaking with her frequently made her feel confident about our relationship. Now to keep it clear, we weren't together but we had a bond that was memorable and unbreakable. We shared something together that we would never let go, but I wasn't being honest about everything. I couldn't help but ask her to step away and have a conversation with me. The look in her eyes was a look of confusion, fear, anger, and dismay. Even though things were the way they were, I still held the utmost respect for this divine creature. So what if we went our separate ways physically, but emotionally we always stayed connected. With that being said a conversation had to be had regardless.

The first thing I did was hug her tightly and passionately. That moment didn't matter because all the memories we shared came rushing back into existence. I felt normal and whole. This was the only sense of normalcy I'd had in a very long time.

Though we had stepped away, our connection and vibe caught the attention of my current girlfriend. I was then forced to introduce the two hoping and praying my best friend would play the naive role for the sake of my parents and my current girlfriend. But things got really awkward really fast.

Upon introducing the two, their words became sarcastic and fowl towards each other. Questions were asked, things were assumed and said. Yelling came in effect and attention was drawn to the corner of the room we were occupying. What we thought would be a friendly conversation turned into jealous, hateful, disappointing, and envious cat fight.

My parents and their guests heard the conflict raging, stepping in to intervened. It was absolutely no stopping the two. At this moment, my secret lifestyle was revealed to everyone watching. My parents became immediately upset. I didn't know if it was from me not being honest with them from the beginning or if it was because of who I was or had become. The argument was broken up by house guests. But I felt so angry and deceived by my so-called best friend, now my ex-best friend.

Here it comes…

Here is the moment of truth!…
"Well hello," my ex said.

Now you know I greeted in return and even more so with an affectionate hug. I introduced the two girls, nervous as hell. They gave each other that look of 'yeah I know who you are or at least who you could be' cause in their own way, they both knew me. I wasn't a player, I was confused. Being in same sex relationships,you can easily confuse the friendship part. It can be confusing in trying to separate lovers from simple friends. In heterosexual relationships it's a friendship, but it's still a subconscious divide. More jealousy comes about in homosexual relationships because it's same sex. You never know who's just the friend and who can be the potential lover.

LIFE HAPPENS

The girls disappeared in different directions to cool down, so I thought. I found myself explaining myself and crying hysterically because everyone demanded an explanation. The toy-boy type they thought I was and just going through a phase was actually an excuse for who I really am.

Moments later, running up the hallway of my parent's home was my new girlfriend with a mace can in her hands spraying the room. Everyone began covering their faces and eyes while screaming for her to put that away. Scrambling all around to avoid contact with the chemical, my mom stepped too far back and fell, hitting her head on the corner of a marble table. I couldn't believe how out of hand this had all gotten. I was so afraid and worried. My mom was knocked unconscious with blood gushing from a nickel sized hole in her head. We called the ambulance and I couldn't stop thinking of how this was all my fault. Only if I had been honest and not tried to be someone I wasn't to make everyone else happy and myself miserable. I hide my true self from everyone I loved in fear of being judged. I didn't display the same confidence I portrayed. *Who was I?* I found myself right back at the beginning of this image transition. Confused and hurt.

LIFE HAPPENS

My mom received about six staples in her head and now she's not able to work, travel or anything. I blamed myself for it all. My dad is so stressed out because now he really realizes how much of a backbone my mom was for him and the family.

My girlfriend and my best friend no longer play any part in my life. They left because of the lies. My family forgives me, but forgetting isn't in the near future for any of us. I had to drop out of school to help my dad with bills and help assist with taking care of my mom. My life has just gone downhill due to the lack of truth, and the confidence in the understanding of my family.

LIFE HAPPENS

I had no choice but except responsibility for my deceiving actions. All I have at this point is my word. My word on being ME. My word on loving ME. My word on building my self-esteem. When there is such lack of communication in your life, you began to live inside your own head full of misinformation. It's unfortunate because mind readers are rare and misconception comes very easy when things and thoughts of others are assumed without question. I live with the fact every day that all of this could have been avoided. Then to make peace with myself and to begin forgiving myself, I understand God puts things in perspective unknowingly to man. I

LIFE HAPPENS

hate the path I chose for myself but I also wonder, if the conclusion had been happily ever after, would I still feel the same? Probably not, but that's the craziness about life, because I'll never know. My prayers for strength to move forward and for confidence to be me is all I'm left with and sometimes all you need.

Chapter 6
Closing Notes

Life Happens.....To the Best of Us

Chapter 6

Closing Notes

Believing that "Life Happens.......To the Best of Us"

Life Happens......To the Best of Us is a story about choices, tests, mistakes, and the deliverance from evil. This book is written up of several short stories straight to the point and meant to exemplify the beginning and ending of works of faith. So many people in the world have experienced so many interesting choices; some caused happy endings, others,not so happy endings and moments of truth based on their decision making. As soon as you are born into this world, "Life Happened" to you. No matter if you were born with a silver spoon in your mouth, in poverty, or born into trust fund inheritance, it is the best of you whom get challenged with the decisions you make for yourself that affect you and those around you.

LIFE HAPPENS

No one in this world wants to be robbed of their choices, options, and/or reasoning. No one inspires to be deprived of choices by others making choices for them through lies, deceit, or withheld information. So much of truth is not told, and as a result of that, the world continues to go down a road of destruction, distraction, and sin.

God is a forgiving God, and this is recited in all religions across the nation, but if that is the truth they live by then why the lies that cover the truth and hinder our growth as a nation and a people. A great number of educators have been removed from the walks of the world and only left words in the face of those who have carried on that fight for knowledge and justice. It seems as though, as soon as truth is told, they move forth with God to the other side of life and we as people are only left with that little education to figure out the rest on our own.

I sometimes wonder if that fact is the reason why the not so political people, just us everyday folks, refuse to live in truth that can harm friendships, relationships, families, marriages, etc. So many folks grew up with the tradition of leaving secrets under the roofs of households that only cause generational curses. I think it was a misconception of what wasn't any and everyone's business. The way

LIFE HAPPENS

we were taught not to question God, we were also taught not to question our parents in understanding some things that were too emotionally challenging or difficult for them to answer or explain. This assumption doesn't apply to all person's growth or past upbringings, but it does apply to a great percentage of everyday people.

As many statistics show, physical and/or mental abuse is learned behavior that had been directed to stay hidden behind the doors of homes. Women have used the excuse of staying in their failed relationships for financial assistance, which in fact can be truthful, but with lost self-esteem, those women believe they are not capable of providing for the large families they birthed without the help of a man, abusive or not. Some are embarrassed to cry out for help after creating such story book lifestyles for themselves. When in reality they are creating more of a mess and more mental destruction, not only for themselves but for the kids who are witnessing this behavior.

Long term marriages of 20, 30, 40 years aren't always marriages built of love, respect, trust, and friendships with communication that we grew up idolizing, some were actually business and comfort arrangements. I'm going out on a limb to discuss this, but some

LIFE HAPPENS

marriages were only arranged because of the reproduction of kids and the financial help needed to provide for and be around for those kids daily. I've met women and men who have grown in houses of marriages of those whom live separate lives. The woman wasn't allowed to be part of the man's recreational time. She was confined to the home and taking care of the household duties. Yes, men today find it exciting to say that their mom was home when they came home from school as kids and dinner awaited them, but what they fail to say is that those men worked hard too, unlike some men do today.

LIFE HAPPENS

In this day and age it takes two to create a comfortable household. with each assisting in finances, housework, and raising the kids. Stress is taken out of the home a little more with that kind of care and team work. Though some folks admired what they thought they saw, they rarely saw the hugs, kisses, date night, soft communication between their parents, and today that's what most people want; best friends forever.

People want to know that their relationship fight wasn't for nothing. They want to grow old together, get sick together, lose their minds together, and have a memory together that only they share of deepest darkest secrets. The thriving black marriages that have made it and beat all odds when fighting dysfunctional black love and became the epitome of black love should stand proud to show the world and upcoming generations that it can become a reality.

For those who experienced witnessing true love, I pray they teach not only their kids, but the generations ahead the secrets of affection. Know that God shall always come first in your lives, homes, relationships. Our young black people should not grow up settling to become single parents, criminals, broken households, and bastards. We are so much more worthy as a people. Life is meant to exceed tests to result in testimonies, learned lessons to share with anyone who'll listen to reason. Life is not meant to be lived bottled in for only one's selfish teachings.

In my opinion, God delivers us from evil situations to allow us to inspire hope, faith, trust in Him, and belief in those who may think situations are hopeless and they are helpless. Know that nothing is hopeless nor helpless in God's timing. In all fairness, He doesn't give up on you and He doesn't expect for you to give up on Him. Some prayers come with huge tests. Some successes come with premeditated failures, in order for your successes to better be

LIFE HAPPENS

appreciated. If you think about it, you're more mindful of the mishandling of blessings you have to work extremely hard for rather than those that came extremely easy or are handed to you. The basis of it all is to work on your communication skills with one another. Be more receiving of lost truth left in the drawer of your memories. Some parts of your past have been stored on a dusty shelf, but it won't ever go away. You find yourself being a lost soul. The disappearance of who you are can resurface at anytime in your life. You may think you have lived a great life and had it all together, until one day your unresolved past comes back into your life to haunt you.

LIFE HAPPENS

Waiting on that time in my opinion can only lead to mental illnesses. Sometimes there's no clarity because what you thought you had under control was actually a fictional way of living for you. If you're faced with a mental or emotional beating at 20 years old for example, deal with it at 20 years old. Don't bring so much pain of your past into your future if you can help it. It's a little different in a child's case, but just be opened to listened to their hurt and truth even if it hurts you. It can only began healing towards a future of less emotional baggage which isn't fair to those who enter your lives to share your days.

LIFE HAPPENS

When those memories began to resurface, who's to say that those who could share those memories to give you closure will even be alive still. Then you find yourself thinking hurtful and unforgiving thoughts to see those love ones again to make you whole again. Life is a cycle, what you past up mentally will eventually show face again, whether through memorabilia or seeing it through the actions or behavior of your kids. I have so much life to live ahead of me, but my attribute is that I find life to be so intriguing, I don't want to miss a beat of it's lessons. I think that just a few more words and a little more attention could began changing the generation. Back in the day the saying was, "Sticks and stones may break my bones, but words will never hurt me". Where are those strong minded people today? Because in this world, words are taking lives, ruining families and relationships, and due to just that the world becomes more of fiction until the truth finds itself. Either way it ends horribly.

My choice, on the other hand, is to have no fear and tell my truth. Whether that is to have my truth corrected into real truth or made known of what I can't be manipulated into covering up for someone else's feelings. Though I may be protecting the ones I love or loved, how can that ever be my healing towards a free kind of me? In taking that stand, I think molestation will stop with you before carrying on to your children. I think the domestic abuse will stop with you when you put your foot down rather than carrying on that behavior to your children. Let us began and try being more truthful. Stop covering for the irresponsible parent and let it be seen to the child, rather than tell stories of excuses why they aren't doing their part. Don't add any more destruction to the already failed relationships, but quit enabling the absentee. Teach your kids who not to be without destroying their names, let God handle their lessons and punishments. Stop pretending to be someone you're not to appease to the liking of everyone else who you can never please anyway. If we all live for ourselves and what makes us happier as more peaceful people, we will be in a better emotional place to be where we need to be to help assist in making changes to our world. I inspire to change the minds of those who find themselves lost, whether that be because of losing a love one by marriage or death. It's sad to say but along with life's accomplishments comes loses. Some people, places, or things are to be sacrificed for a better you and/or a better life. I want the young mothers and fathers who become parents too soon before accomplishing their goals to continue to push forward and pray harder. It can happen for you and believe that it will happen for you to get your lives right where you aspire them to be. All things are possible through Christ or whatever or whomever you believe in. "BELIEF" is the key word and emotional/spiritual action to be greater than you can ever imagine for yourself. If you don't exercise that action in you then who will? It doesn't matter if you're a Saint or Sinner, in other words good or bad, big or small, short or tall, regardless of however you chose to live it there will always be tests, let downs, disappointments, and mistakes. As long as you can take in constructive criticism and truth to become better/wiser, and learn from your heartaches, you can always find forgiveness. Each day of blessed air you breathe gives you an opportunity to start over. The best part of it all is that as long as you continue to choose life and live it, then...

Life Happens...To the Best of Us!!!

"LIFE PLANS"

"For I know the plans I have for you," declares the Lord, "plans to prosper you and not to harm you, plans to give you hope and a future."

Jeremiah 29:11

LIFE HAPPENS

SPEND SOME TIME WITH GOD ASKING FOR HIS DIRECTION AND HIS GUIDANCE

LIFE HAPPENS.....

To the Best of Us

Contact Info:

Email: dorianbaham@gmail.com

Blog: dorianbaham.weebly.com

Facebook: Dorian Baham

Instagram: msdoeoriginalpmr

"Never Judge A Book By The Cover"
By: Dorian Baham

Is Available on Amazon, Kindle, Community Book Store located in

LIFE HAPPENS

New Orleans, La., Barnes & Nobles Book Store, and everywhere at your fingertips.

Dorian Baham is a salon owner of "The Original Picture Me Rollin' Salon

Located at 10040 Read I-10 Service Road in New Orleans, La 70127.

This business is a family based, professional environment and has been for 20 years.

If ever in the New Orleans area please feel free to stop by for a hair care service or even an autographed copy of either book written by Author Dorian Baham.

Google Dorian Baham to stay informed of all her endeavors.

LIFE HAPPENS...

To the Best of Us

About The Author

Dorian Baham is a new-found author who has exercised her talent by writing stories of real life. As a result of her previous book, "**Never Judge a Book by the Cover**" she received such awesome feedback of testimonial stories of everyday people. Dorian Baham decides to use those testimonies and combine them to create such an intriguing story. Life has its way of presenting us all with unexpected turns. Once we figure we have it all, then God shows us different. Her bio in "**Never Judge a Book by the Cover**" opened up so many doors of faith, confidence, opportunities, strength, self-worth and courage for so many others. People found her to be such a strengthened role model for so many upcoming authors with lost or hidden stories skin deep. Her motto is "Everyone Has a Book in Them" It's just that we have to find it within ourselves to share it. The only real therapy to life and perseverance is to open up about "YOUR TRUTH." Confronting one's past can better allow peace, harmony, and happiness into their future. From experiences in her own life; she then realizes that the plans of man aren't

LIFE HAPPENS

the same plan of "THE MAN", our Father God. At that point in your life, you don't have a pity party nor beat yourself up. You stay prayed up, understand that there is a greater plan for you and believe in it, because in all actuality, no matter the situation or choice "**LIFE HAPPENS**."

ENJOY YOUR READ AND
REMEMBER

LIFE HAPPENS...

To the Best of Us

LIFE HAPPENS

Author Dorian Baham

Author of : Never Judge A Book by the Cover

Never Judge A Book By The Cover

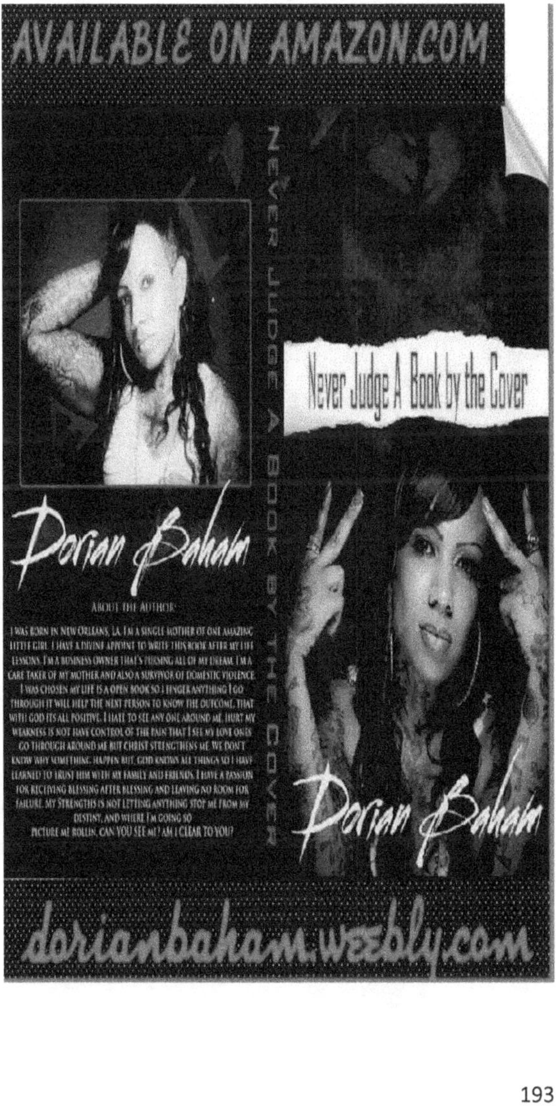

Dorian's Heartbeat

Dorian Baham:

The Business Woman

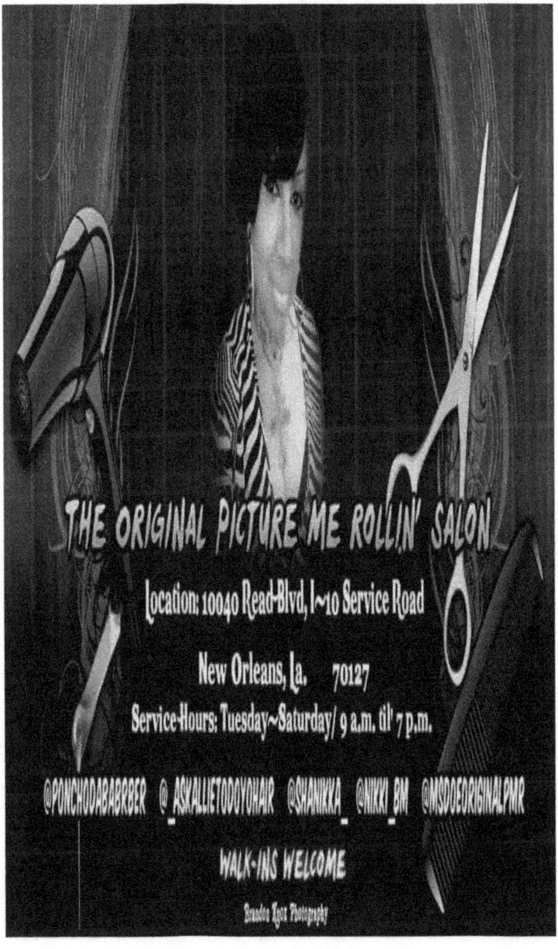

DOWNSOUTH HOLLYWOOD
T.V. SHOW
BAYOU DIVAS
DORIAN BAHAM: DORIANBAHAM@GMAIL.COM
RESHAUNDA BLANKS: (504) 621-8656
WUPL.TV
@MSDOEORIGINALPMR
@NEKELL_
Brandon Knox Photography

Dorian Baham:

The Volunteer

Volunteering with the Homeless

LIFE HAPPENS

LIFE HAPPENS

LIFE HAPPENS

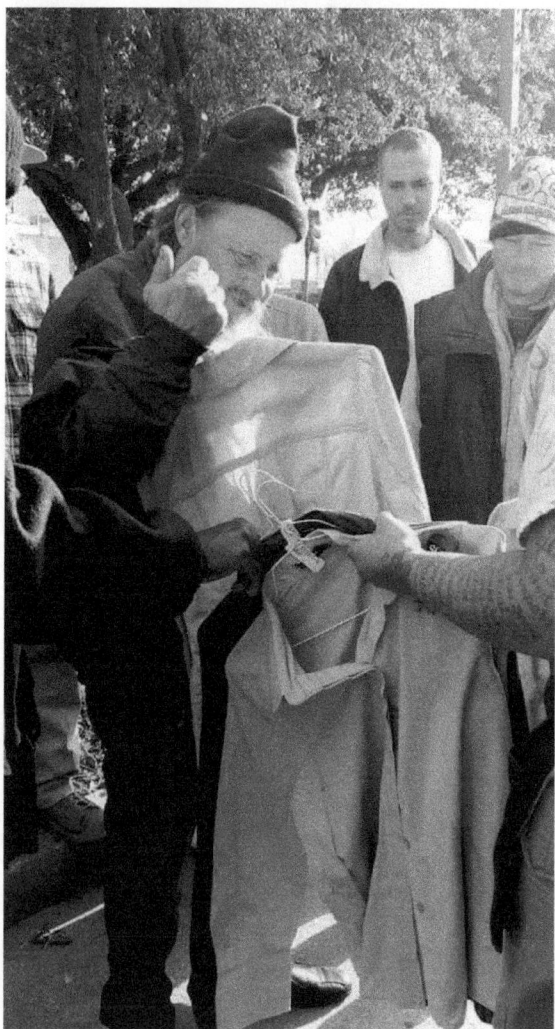

Partial proceeds from all Dorian's books go to her mission "A Little Help Gives A Lot of Hope"